# The *Promise* of WATER

## The Garrison Diversion Project

The
Promise
of
WATER

The Garrison Diversion Project

# Photographs by Wayne Gudmundson

## Essay by Robert Silberman

**The Promise of Water**
The Garrison Diversion Project

Graphic Design:
Allen Sheets Graphic Design

Pre Press and Printing:
Pettit Network Inc., Afton MN

Printed in China

Softcover ISBN: 0-911042-58-X
Hardcover ISBN: 0-911042-59-8

Library of Congress Control Number: 2002107054

*Institute for Regional Studies*
*NDSU*

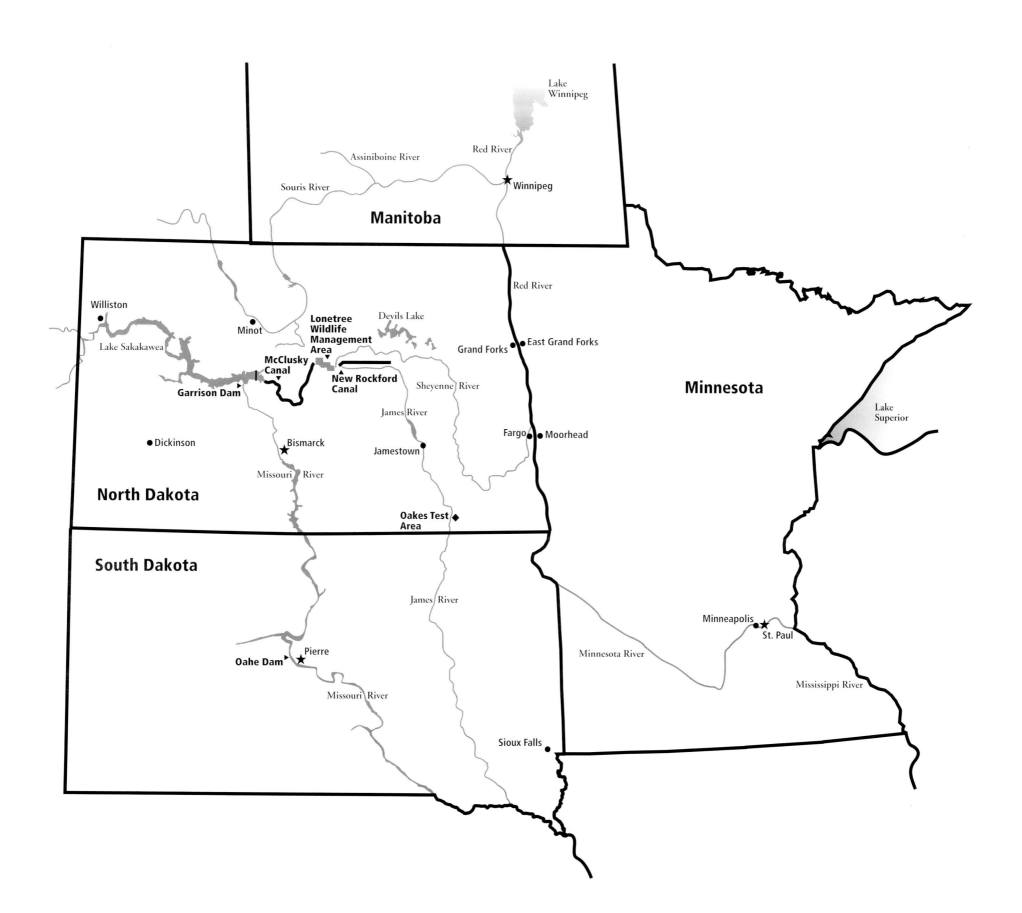

*Best of all things is water.*

PINDAR

*Whiskey is for drinking,
and water is for fighting about.*

MARK TWAIN

# The Promise and Politics of Water

## by Robert Silberman

**I** The Garrison Diversion Project has been a controversial political issue in North Dakota for decades. It has passed through many different versions, but all have one thing in common: the diversion of Missouri River water for use within North Dakota. More than a half billion dollars already have been spent, and a comparable amount is being sought to bring the project to completion. The landscape has been transformed by pumping stations and other large-scale waterworks, along with more than one hundred twenty miles of canals. But not a drop of water has flowed from the Missouri to the James and Sheyenne rivers, and from them into what is now the major proposed destination, the Red River of the North.

The idea of diverting Missouri River water arose along with North Dakota statehood. On August 5, 1889, the famous explorer and scientist John Wesley Powell, then director of the

U.S. Geological Survey, addressed the state constitutional convention in Bismarck. He urged North Dakotans to "look the thing squarely in the face" and consider diverting the Missouri for irrigation purposes. He said that was necessary because of generally inadequate rainfall in the western and central sections of the state and occasional drought in the eastern. "All other wealth," Powell declared, "falls into insignificance compared with that which is to come from these lands from the pouring on them of the running streams of this country" (Wilkins, 95).

By the end of the nineteenth century, Donald Worster writes in *Rivers of Empire*, "irrigation had become a veritable crusade, urged on moral, patriotic, religious, economic, and scientific grounds" (114). The convention sent a request to Congress to consider a plan to construct a canal across the state that would bring water for irrigation from the Missouri in Montana to the Red River of the North. The proposal was turned down as infeasible. But the idea of diverting water

*County Road 20 near Devils Lake under two feet of water, July 1997.*

in support of irrigation rather than letting it flow by unused has remained alive ever since.

The next notable proposal for a diversion of water from the Missouri came as the result of a local problem not related to irrigation: in the 1920s the water level in Devils Lake was declining. That led Sivert W. Thompson, a lawyer and secretary of the Devils Lake Chamber of Commerce, to make diverting water into Devils Lake a personal crusade. He organized the Missouri River Diversion Association in 1924 and prepared the way for proposals such as a 1927 plan that required a thirty-mile-long tunnel crossing the Continental Divide. Ironically, the main provocation for action early in the twentieth century, the water level of Devils Lake, which fell more than fifteen feet between 1901 and 1933, rose more than twenty feet at the end of the century and is now disastrously high, with many houses lost and more threatened. As recently as 1991, a proposal called for an inlet to Devils Lake. In a proposal from 2000, that was changed to an inlet/outlet. An outlet is what is apparently needed now, although drained waters could cause problems elsewhere and a lowered water level might increase the salinity of the lake, spoiling the fishing. And the precipitation pendulum could always swing the other way, causing the water level to drop and making an inlet once again necessary.

*Aerial view of Garrison Dam and Lake Sakakawea, 1996.*

The plight of Devils Lake alone might not have led to any action. In North Dakota, water was not at first regarded as a general problem, even though the average annual precipitation is sixteen inches for the state, with less in the western part and more in the eastern. The railroad companies had brought newcomers to the high plains with promises of boom times, supported by the theory that "rain follows the plow" (i.e., rainfall is increased by agricultural development and population growth). This notion took on the semblance of truth after the Civil War and into the 1870s, a period of unusually high rainfall. But in the final decades of the century rainfall reverted to more typical levels, the claims of the promoters were shown to rest not on physics but on faith, and thousands of people left their homesteads.

North Dakota, settled relatively late in the century, survived that crisis because the eastern part of the state could do extremely well in average times and dry-land-farming techniques could sustain farms in the other areas. The Great Depression and Dust Bowl period, a time of economic crisis coinciding with another move below historical norms for precipitation and into extreme drought, raised the water issue once again. During the Depression, one-third of the farms in North Dakota suffered foreclosure, and half the state's residents were on some kind of government subsidy. More than one hundred twenty thousand residents left the state; forty-three of its fifty-three counties lost population. At one point, no water flowed in the Red River at Fargo for 165 days.

Yet the proposal for diversion of the Missouri languished until circumstances outside the borders of North Dakota provided an opportunity for it to gain political support. First, flooding in cities such as Omaha, Kansas City, and St. Louis had become intolerable. Pressure from downriver states was crucial for passage of legislation. Second, the New Deal brought a new willingness in Washington to undertake large-scale public works programs that went beyond individual states to address whole river basins, as in the Tennessee Valley Authority and Columbia River projects.

The Fort Peck Dam in Montana was completed in 1940, the first dam along the main-stem Missouri. But the proposed government program for the river blurred the line between various emphases: flood control, irrigation, and power generation. As a result, there was a titanic struggle between the U.S. Army Corps of Engineers and the U.S. Bureau of Reclamation. After a bureaucratic deadlock—and immense and destructive floods in both 1942 and 1943—separate plans put forward by the two competing bureaucracies were merged, no doubt to avoid the threat that control of the river would be given to a new federal agency and leave the old agencies, as it were, high and dry. Heralded as a compromise, the outcome was no compromise at all: both sides had their wishes granted. There were to be dams and reservoirs that would support hydroelectric and irrigation projects, the traditional concerns of the Bureau of Reclamation, as well as flood control and navigation projects, the bailiwick of the Corps of Engineers. Franklin Delano Roosevelt signed the Flood Control Act into law on December 22, 1944. The president of the National Farmers Union, which had supported the idea of a "Missouri Valley Authority" in part because of distrust of the Corps and the Bureau, labeled the so-called compromise a "loveless, shotgun marriage" (Doemel, 19).

The resolution of the bureaucratic warfare helped lead to the construction of the Garrison Dam, completed in 1953, the prologue to the Garrison Diversion Project. President Dwight D. Eisenhower attended the completion ceremonies. To create the dam and the two hundred-mile-long Lake Sakakawea it produced, it was necessary for the state—and the Fort Berthold Indian Reservation, which was cut in two by the reservoir—to surrender land adjacent to the river. This has been the main point of contention ever since. North Dakota politicians invariably claim entitlement to redress and employ terms such as "contractual agreement," although no formal agreement was ever signed. "Politics ain't bean bag," Finley Peter Dunne's Mr. Dooley observed (Dunne, 3); to which he might have added, "So make sure you get everything in writing." Colorado made certain an agreement in a comparable situation was included in the enabling legislation. South Dakota, like North Dakota caught without such a defense, made a similar claim for the reservoir behind the Oahe Dam, another project arising from the Flood Control Act. A review found the South Dakota claim to be based upon a probable "political understanding" but no evidence of "a formal legal commitment" (Carrels, 169). In any event, the claim by North Dakota politicians that the surrender of lands for the Garrison Dam and reservoir incurred a federal obligation led to the idea that compensation should be paid in the form of a Missouri River diversion project.

*Billboard erected on Ben Schatz's farm next to the McClusky Canal, 1972.*

After the construction of the Fort Peck Dam, there was a proposal to divert water from its reservoir to 1.275 million acres in northwest North Dakota. That land proved unsuitable for irrigation. The original proposal for what came to be known as the Garrison Diversion Project, following from the construction of the Garrison Dam, was for a water system extending to the north-central part of the state, where a canal was to feed the Souris River; to the northeast, with Devils Lake as a recipient; and to the southeast, where water would be brought by the James. The irrigation plans have repeatedly been cut back, leaving a tiny remnant of the original grand design. The latest proposal includes only the maintenance of the five thousand-acre Oakes Test Area and two small parcels on Indian land. Opponents fear irrigation may be developed by the state on a more significant scale if and when the main diversion project is completed. For their part, diversion proponents have attempted to preserve the option of large-scale irrigation. In December 1998 a new organization, the North Dakota Irrigation Caucus, was formed to continue irrigation advocacy.

The original figures for the Garrison Diversion irrigation, it turns out, were arrived at through wishful thinking, since once again much of the acreage proposed for irrigation proved unsuitable. What is called a "windshield survey" was apparently employed at times, with the Bureau of Reclamation agents driving down the road and eyeballing the land on either side, then designating areas without deigning to perform adequate soil tests. Accompanying such estimates of potential irrigation acreage have been equally questionable estimates of the value of irrigation in terms of population increases, new farms and factories, and overall economic benefits. In 1942 Kenneth W. Simons, editor of the *Bismarck Tribune* and chairman of the Irrigation Committee of the Water Conservation Commission, said, "If North Dakota is to

have a population of two million persons with jobs and businesses for all, the best opportunity in this generation lies in the development of her water resources" (Wilkins, 97). That remains a big "if": the state's population has never approached one million.

The projected cost to introduce irrigation often clashed with the projected benefits, especially because over the decades the proposed irrigation was limited to far fewer acres while the costs of the project—due only in part to inflation—became ever greater. Only twelve hundred to fifteen hundred farms would be direct beneficiaries of a program that would cost hundreds of millions of dollars. In 1959 the U.S. Bureau of the Budget opposed the Garrison proposal because of cost. Irrigation might lead to greater crop diversification and yields, but its value became questionable when the subsidies were so great, the repayments so small, the cost to individual farmers so large, and the rewards so uncertain. By the 1970s, farm subsidies had removed millions of acres in North Dakota from cultivation to limit over-production and bolster prices. That raised a question about irrigating acreage at great expense, especially when the land proposed for irrigation was already productive cropland. Similarly, where the original plan saw few problems with eliminating wildlife habitat, the increasing strength of the environmental movement made the possible loss of key areas such as Kraft Slough, a 950-acre wetland, a rallying-point for opponents. Project proposals have included compensatory measures, but that has produced fierce contention over the measurement of lost and replacement acreage and over the need to take productive farmland as mitigation under a no-net-loss wetlands policy.

Even Floyd Dominy, the formidable commissioner of the Bureau of Reclamation at the height of its power, and a man who in general never met a river he didn't want to dam or a water project he didn't want to undertake, privately acknowledged in 1955 when he was chief of the Irrigation Division "the impropriety and damn foolishness involved in the construction of irrigation projects in relatively good dry land areas" (Reisner, 192). He noted that such projects came about because local towns and businessmen wanted them: "They could see themselves growing fat on large-scale construction payrolls. They could see something to be gained by increasing the number of farm families in their service area. Like the usual selfish citizen they were willing to accept this increase to their personal larder without thought as to the burden to be placed on the Federal tax payer." As the late Marc Reisner remarks in *Cadillac Desert*, his acerbic, devastating study of water policies and practices in the American West, Dominy "managed to overcome such scruples after he was appointed commissioner" (192).

The Garrison Dam and the Garrison Diversion Project benefited for many years from what Robert Gottlieb has referred to in *A Life of Its Own* as "the iron triangle" at the heart of water development in the twentieth-century United States, a "three-way interlocking network of interests" formed by Congress, the water agencies, and the local water industry groups (47). Through the 1960s, this system virtually guaranteed that projects were approved. Gottlieb recounts that one committee chairman boasted, "There is something here for everybody" (48). The practice known as "logrolling" meant that by an unspoken rule legislators did not attack water projects in other districts. During key years when Garrison was under consideration, both North Dakota senators sat on the Appropriations Committee. The North Dakota delegation, always united behind the Garrison project, therefore had unusual power. In an unguarded moment, Senator Quentin Burdick said: "Hell, if it wasn't for the Senate it would have died years ago. We pass it by a good margin in the Senate every time and then we go to conference committee. They generally have zero [support] from the House. . . . We just shoulder the damn conferees around until we can make them agree with us" (Pearson, 8).

This political situation was the background in the post–World War II period for the revival of the Missouri River diversion proposal. In 1957 the Garrison Conservancy District was established by the North Dakota legislature; that enabled taxation for the program within a twenty-five- (later twenty-six-) county area. The initial phase of construction of the Garrison Diversion Unit was authorized by the federal government in 1965 after failed attempts in 1957, 1960, 1963, and 1964. The formal groundbreaking ceremony for the Snake Creek Pumping Station that would move water from Lake Sakakawea behind the Garrison Dam into Lake Audubon as a holding reservoir before it was sent down the McClusky Canal took place on July 14, 1968, with Vice-President Hubert Humphrey as the speaker. The 73.6-mile-long canal was built between 1969 and 1976. Even as social unrest over civil rights and the Vietnam War clouded the picture, the decades after mid-century were marked by immense government

*Meeting of the Garrison Diversion Unit Conference in the office of Senator Milton R. Young (sixth from right), Washington, D.C., February 19, 1954.*

projects such as the interstate highway system and public-private initiatives such as the nuclear power industry that aroused no widespread civilian concern. There was as yet little of the antigovernment libertarian spirit identified with Ronald Reagan and the Sagebrush Rebellion, or the "not in my backyard" syndrome.

The Garrison Diversion Project was at first supported by the overwhelming majority of the population. As Elwyn Robinson noted in his *History of North Dakota*, "No one in North Dakota publicly questioned the benefits of diversion, any more than he would motherhood, virtue, or patriotism" (465). This is not surprising. The politicians, the major newspapers, and the business community all proclaimed the diversion idea an unqualified good. Moreover, the project sites were stretched out along a narrow strip in sparsely populated rural areas, and therefore removed from the daily experience of most citizens.

The construction of the McClusky Canal, although accomplished with relatively little opposition, especially at first, ultimately aroused resistance. There are many horror stories of callous treatment by Bureau of Reclamation agents of farmers whose land was taken for right-of-way. When a farmer complained that his farm would be cut into three parts by the canal and he would have to reduce his cattle herd by a third, he was told: "To us you're just a dot on the map. When you get in the way, we move you" (Carrels, 70). He was so angered that he put up a billboard on his land in protest. The high-pressure tactics, low purchase prices, lack of concern with relocation assistance, unwillingness to present plans that would identify those affected by future developments, and crude insensitivity to the farmers might now appear unimaginable. At the time, such actions were a rude awakening, as landowners came to realize just how much their lives and livelihoods were being affected by the Garrison Diversion Project. In a booklet published by the Bureau of Reclamation to convince landowners along the New Rockford Canal (another segment in the diversion plan) to sell their land without protest, the question, "Why must my land be acquired?" is answered this way:

EVERY LANDOWNER could ask this same question. No one likes to be told that he must do something, but someone's property must be acquired in the public interest or the development of our country would come to a standstill. It is unfortunate that a few persons must be inconvenienced for the welfare of all, but this happens to each of us, in one way or another, every day. This is the price of progress. It is inevitable in the advancement of society ["Procedures for the Purchase of Land and Right of Way," 5].

It must have infuriated property owners to be told that the loss of their land was "unfortunate" but "inevitable," an inconvenience no different from what happens to all citizens, "in one way or another, every day."

During the critical period when the McClusky and New Rockford canals were being constructed, the leader of the opposition was Richard Madson. An associate editor of the *North Dakota Union Farmer*, in 1972 he was assigned to investigate the treatment of farmers along the McClusky in response to a directive from the Farmers Union board of governors, which had received complaints from McLean County. He was, in his own words, "shocked and outraged" by what he observed. The article reporting on the investigation findings, "Garrison Diversion: Rumblings on the Ditch," was published in July 1972. But the organization still officially supported the project; Madson was forced to leave the staff. A short time later, on August 3, Glen Sherwood, the U.S. Fish and Wildlife Service biologist who had resigned to speak freely against the Garrison project and was about to publish a polemic against it, *New Wounds for Old Prairies*, gave a speech at a Farmers Union meeting held at the town hall in Turtle Lake. Afterward some of those present, upset by the organization's refusal to consider opposition to the project, formed a group of thirty-one members, contributing ten dollars each. They grandly named themselves the Committee to Save North Dakota. Madson became the leader, supported by a dedicated corps of farmers, ranchers, conservationists, and other citizens. Membership eventually reached five hundred.

At the height of the controversy, in the late 1970s and early 1980s, Madson worked for the Audubon Society out of a field office in Jamestown, North Dakota, and therefore could devote himself to the fight against Garrison, just as the pro-Garrison politicians and Conservancy District employees could as part of their jobs work on behalf of the project. Audubon Society support, and that of other environmental organizations such as the National

Board of Directors of the Committee to Save North Dakota (Richard Madson, third from right in back row), 1973.

Wildlife Foundation and the Izaak Walton League, proved important to the opposition in many ways, as when an article appeared in *Audubon* magazine in 1975 entitled "Dr. Strangelove Builds a Canal" (Josephy). It reached an audience far beyond the borders of North Dakota, as did other media coverage, including a *Reader's Digest* article, "Half a Billion Dollars down the Drain," which referred to the project as "lunatic" and "an average run-of-the-mill worthless project" (Miller, 148, 143).

Madson describes himself at that time as "brash." He became a gadfly to the project's advocates with his repeated calls for a public debate and his demand for a moratorium on Garrison construction. The refrain of Madson and the opposition was not "Stop Garrison" but "Study Garrison," along with an insistence that they only wanted to return the project to its original purpose, described in nicely vague terms as "to help small farmers, help stabilize the economy, and help wildlife." Project proponents, however, knew that funding for public works was always vulnerable to changing economic circumstances and shifts in the political winds: a delay could prove fatal. At a time when "generation gap" was a cultural commonplace, the differences in age, style, and outlook between Madson and Senator Milton R. Young, perhaps Garrison's leading booster, took on a symbolic aspect. The North Dakota establishment was not used to being challenged in such direct, relentless, and effective fashion.

The Committee to Save North Dakota used some ingenious tactics. In addition to the billboard, there was a newspaper ad that included a list of proposed Garrison Diversion land acquisitions that had been kept secret by the Bureau of Reclamation, and asked readers whether, when their children were ready to take over, they would still have land to farm. There were also bumper stickers with slogans such as "Small farmers out—as Diversion comes in?" and "Garrison Diversion?: When They Speak of the Benefits—Ask of the Costs!" When Young termed opponents "outside environmental extremists"—Madson was born in Minnesota and educated in South Dakota—a farmer from the Committee was recruited to appear in bib overalls at a press conference and say, "I oppose the Garrison Diversion, and I'm no outside environmental extremist."

Whatever the specifics of the North Dakota situation, the conflict over the Garrison project was typical of battles over water policy in the United States during the 1970s.

A combination of environmentalism, fiscal conservatism, and tension over perceived funding inequities between regions led to an attack on pork barrel business as usual. On January 1, 1970, President Richard Nixon signed into law the National Environmental Policy Act, which required environmental impact statements; they became a major tool for environmentalists. Garrison opponents were quick to use the new legislation to challenge the project in a series of legal actions.

The most important support for the Committee to Save North Dakota and its allies, and a decisive new element in the political contest, came from the Canadian government. In 1973 it requested a moratorium on the project under the Boundary Waters Treaty of 1909. It filed a formal protest on two grounds, both reinforced in a 1977 report from the International Joint Commission, a U.S.-Canadian group created by the treaty to address water issues. First, there was concern about the possibility that return flows—the drainage from irrigated fields—would reach Canada. That danger eventually led to the deletion of the proposed Velva Canal (which would have been eighty-four miles long) and Souris River irrigation area (at more than one hundred thousand acres, the largest section of the entire project) in north-central North Dakota. Second, there was concern about biota, that is, living matter such as fish, fish eggs, and pathogens. Bringing Missouri River water to the Red River would combine water from the Missouri River Basin with water flowing to Hudson Bay. The Canadians objected to what they perceived as a threat to fisheries in Lake Winnebago and elsewhere, and to this day they remain unconvinced by a series of studies and proposals that argue the water could be effectively filtered.

In 1977 President Jimmy Carter deleted nineteen water projects from the 1978 fiscal year budget in an attempt to fulfill campaign promises to cut down on governmental waste and be pro-environment. The Garrison Diversion was on the so-called hit list. U.S. Secretary of the Interior Cecil Andrus described Garrison as "the dog" of all water projects (Russell, 10), yet he warned the president on tactical grounds not to attack the water interests so broadly—to no avail. Infuriated senators from both parties responded by explaining the absolute necessity of funding projects in their districts, while framing their action as a principled defense of congressional privilege against an imperial presidency. In the final 1978 budget Garrison was saved, but with new construction reduced while another study was performed. One victim of the Carter cuts was the Oahe project in South Dakota, another large-scale irrigation endeavor designed to exploit a Missouri River main-stem dam and reservoir. It was defeated because strong local leadership of the opposition, working in a circumscribed area, won control of

the conservancy district board, by law the cosponsor of any federal project. The insurgents refused to sign off on any agreement, foiling the pro-Oahe forces. They were inspired in part by a tour of the McClusky Canal led by Madson as a warning of what might happen should they not organize to resist the Oahe proposal.

In 1982 James Watt, U.S. Secretary of the Interior in the Reagan Administration, voiced his support for the Garrison project. In spite of the policy of cost-sharing between states and the federal government, he said it should be federally funded. But President Reagan announced that he would defer spending and possibly withdraw support for fiscal 1985. After a compromise was struck between North Dakota Senator Mark Andrews and the Audubon Society establishing a review commission, the administration requested $53.5 million for Garrison in a budget proposal. And so, between 1983 and 1991, the forty-four-mile-long New Rockford Canal was built. Twenty-four thousand acres were taken for the right-of-way, but greater consideration was shown to landowners in land acquisition and in construction of cattle-crossings as well as regular bridges to make travel from one side of the canal to the other more convenient.

The opposition could not stop the New Rockford Canal. But it did stop construction of the Lonetree Dam and Reservoir, the central water-holding-and-distribution point for the whole Garrison Diversion Project and the connecting link between the McClusky and New Rockford canals. The land, already taken by the government, was turned into the Lonetree Wildlife Management Area, following a recommendation by the review commission. The commission also recommended reducing the irrigation once more, from 250,000 to 130,000 acres, and eliminating any drainage into Canadian waters and Hudson Bay. The diversion was to focus on municipal water supplies, not irrigation. In 1986 a statement of principles was signed by the governor, the Conservancy District, the Audubon Society, and other interested parties. But even after Congress in 1986 passed the Garrison Diversion Unit Reformulation Act, funding was not forthcoming. Since the completion of the New Rockford Canal the project has been in a state of suspended animation, with continuing efforts by both sides but no decisive action. On site, the main activity has been maintenance of the existing waterworks and canals, a problem made worse because to reduce the land acquired for right-of-way, the banks alongside the canals were made steeper than would have been ideal, causing more erosion and other difficulties (Kelly, 152). Meanwhile, in Washington, a bill passed on December 15, 2000, authorized a new plan but allocated no money, and mandated yet another study, this one to determine whether alternatives to the Garrison Diversion Project exist that might supply water to the cities along the Red River. If all the Garrison reports were laid end to end, they might well stretch from the Garrison Dam to Fargo. In any case, this latest act in the drama means that it could be several years before the issue of actual funding is once again addressed.

| | | | |
|---|---|---|---|
| 1870 | 2,405 | 1940 | 641,935 |
| 1880 | 36,909 | 1950 | 619,636 |
| 1890 | 190,983 | 1960 | 632,446 |
| 1900 | 319,146 | 1970 | 617,792 |
| 1910 | 577,056 | 1980 | 652,717 |
| 1920 | 646,872 | 1990 | 638,800 |
| 1930 | 680,845 | 2000 | 642,200 |

*Resident population of North Dakota • U.S. Census Bureau*

**II** There is no way of knowing whether completion funds for the Garrison Diversion Project will be appropriated. That depends on the economy, on congressional and presidential politics, on international relations with Canada and domestic relationships with bordering and downriver states, and on the play of political forces within North Dakota.

In 2000 the Garrison Diversion Project received $25.2 million in President Bill Clinton's 2002 budget request. More importantly, the $631.5-million authorization bill passed by Congress held out the promise of funding to complete the project. This proposal for what is called the Dakota Water Resources Act—no doubt in part to avoid a name associated with a history of contention, and the terms "boondoggle" and "pork barrel"—has something for almost everybody. Two hundred million dollars are earmarked to bring water to the Red River Valley, but equal amounts go to state grants for municipalities and rural areas and industrial

projects, and to Indian reservation water programs, with the final $31.5 million assigned to the Natural Resources Trust and recreation projects. In American democracy, of such accommodations is consensus constructed.

It is inevitable with a project of this kind that proponents minimize projected costs and possible unhappy consequences and maximize expected benefits while opponents do just the opposite. The current study commission, preparing yet one more report on the alternatives, may or may not lead to a decisive conclusion. In 1975 Mark Andrews, then a congressman, heralded the International Joint Commission as the ultimate adjudicator, saying, "This kind of study is a very exact science." When the 1977 findings did not support his position, he rejected them as "far-fetched and as phony as a $3 bill" (Pearson, 8). A screening mechanism was constructed at a cost of more than $1 million at a turnout on the McClusky Canal, and different proposals have included other possible solutions to the biota problem. But Jay A. Leitch, director of a decade-long study sponsored by project supporters, including the Conservancy District and the Bureau of Reclamation, concluded that Canadian opposition had not lessened and that science alone will never provide "the answer" for policy-makers engaged in the debate over the safety of cross-border flows (Leitch and Tenamoc, 131).

The total project budget for the plan in the mid-1960s was roughly half a billion dollars; at that time, the value of all the state's farmland and buildings was $1.5 billion. The $631.5 million currently proposed to complete the diversion and fund the other projects may appear far less, relatively speaking. Yet for North Dakota the funds would still represent a major infusion of capital. Frederick Jackson Turner, the historian forever identified with his thesis about the role of the frontier in American life, announced in 1903, "The pioneer of the arid regions must be both a capitalist and the protégé of the government" (Worster, 12). Water policies and politics in North Dakota everywhere reveal this doubleness, by accepting a philosophy of individual freedom and the free market along with a practice of reliance upon federal subsidies.

If the project is completed, utopian projections and doomsday predictions alike will be replaced by reality. Estimates will become dollars spent. Plans on paper will be turned into physical transformations of the landscape. The consequences, positive or negative, will be evident. If the project is not given completion funding, some of its goals may be satisfied by other means, but there will be physical ruins and psychological scars. Large amounts of money and effort will have been expended for naught, a possibility that a quarter century and a half billion dollars ago was already part of the debate. In 1974 Senator Milton R. Young said, "It would be unthinkable that this greatest of all North Dakota projects would be stopped now after all the efforts put into it by North Dakota and after approximately $75 million has already been spent." To which Richard Madson countered, "Simply throwing millions of dollars of taxpayers' money into continuation of a project because some money has already been spent is not proper consideration for U.S. taxpayers" ("Young: Diversion in Deep Trouble").

Hindsight, 20-20 as always, shows that the project could have been built to carry the currently proposed amount of water through a pipeline with little or no land acquisition. When construction of the Lonetree Dam and Reservoir was stopped, an alternative was proposed, the Sykeston Canal, to circumvent the Wildlife Management Area and link the McClusky and New Rockford canals. If the entire project moves forward, the Sykeston Canal idea may well be replaced by a pipeline, and pipelines might be used at the eastern end, too, as the final links to Fargo and Grand Forks. Since the project was reformulated in 1986, funding has gone to the Southwest Pipeline, which serves municipal water needs in Dickinson and surrounding communities. The Garrison Conservancy District, always resilient, always adaptable in efforts to maintain itself as more than a maintenance operation, is now stressing the recreational value of project sites and exploring programs that would use the excess capacity of the existing canals (see www.garrisondiv.org). The McClusky Canal, for example, built to carry 1,950 cubic feet of water per second, in the latest proposal would carry only four hundred fifty.

After Floyd Dominy spoke at the annual Chamber of Commerce dinner in Bismarck on February 3, 1966, a newspaper published his speech under the headline, "Dominy: Dakotas on Verge of Greatest Era in History." The piece took up the better part of a page, but only two paragraphs were set in boldface type. In one, Dominy announced that the Garrison project would increase gross farm income by about thirty-three and a third million dollars, yet another in a string of enticing estimates of economic benefits. The other highlighted paragraph contained an even greater promise: "One of the most welcome benefits to be gained from all this reclamation development and its attendant advantages will be the cessation of the outmigration which has plagued the Dakotas in recent years" (Dominy).

There is the basic underlying problem: the difficulty of sustaining population in North Dakota, given its location, its resources, and its climate. Governor John E. Davis, testifying before the congressional Subcommittee on Irrigation and Reclamation on October 30, 1957, was direct about the problem (and used a term soon to achieve fame during the Kennedy Administration): "Irrigation in North Dakota will provide a new frontier for our youth who otherwise must go elsewhere to earn their income" ("Hearings at Devils Lake," 7).

The population issue has always been a factor behind the push to develop the Garrison Diversion. What began primarily as a rural agricultural project, with irrigation described by Vernon Cooper of the Garrison Conservancy District as "the principal purpose" and "backbone" responsible for 80 percent of the costs and 90 percent of the benefits, and with all other purposes "incidental," became primarily an urban program, to support municipal and industrial water supplies (Cooper, 73). What was to serve the central part of the state, in line with John Wesley Powell's view that a man-made remedy was necessary for the shortfall of precipitation there, will now, if funded, emphasize the eastern edge of the state, never mentioned in the original plan. There is pragmatism at work in such shifts, and an unyielding determination to hold onto the claim of entitlement and justify the expenditure of federal dollars by adjusting proposals in any way necessary within the broad framework of water and economic development. If banks, in the famous words of Willie Sutton, are where the money is, water is where, in the federal budget, the available money is, or might be—or used to be. In 1990 the Bush Administration recommended that no funding for the Garrison Diversion be included in the 1991 federal budget. As a result, a bill was introduced in the 1991 North Dakota legislature that would have imposed state sales tax and income tax increases for water projects. The bill did not pass. Neither did a statewide referendum the following year that proposed a sales tax increase for the same purpose; it was defeated by a two-to-one margin. In October 1999 a bill was introduced, passed, and signed into law that would allocate up to $320 million from tobacco-settlement funds for water development over the next twenty-five years, making North Dakota possibly the only state to use such funds in that way.

The federal Dakota Water Resources Act applies a precise economic and political calculus in its allocation of sums to different constituencies. Divisions such as those between Fargo and Grand Forks on one side, Bismarck, Mandan, and Jamestown on the other are masked, for example, behind the always mentioned but questionable declaration of Garrison's value in helping to save the family farm. That cause must be upheld in any statement about the future of North Dakota, but the fate of the state's family farms was not and is not primarily dependent upon the Garrison Diversion Project or the Water Resources Act. Of course, water is essential for farming and farm families. But with irrigation relegated to an insignificant role, the contribution of water to the survival of the family farm is arguably a secondary factor compared to farm subsidies, commodity prices, and other economic variables, as well as the social consequences of rural depopulation.

The history of the Garrison Diversion Project has been described as a key to the North Dakota psyche, a reflection of its sense of victimization and entitlement, its provinciality and resentment of outsiders (Jacobs). It has been viewed as a demonstration of what happens when people subscribe to utopian myths, specifically the belief in human domination of nature and the transformation of a subhumid region into one with the characteristics of land blessed with more precipitation—the kind often left behind when settlers came to North Dakota (Kurian and Bartlett). It is also a case study in the American political process at all levels, from the local and state to the regional and federal, and extending to the international arena as well. The Garrison Diversion proposal, now the Water Resources Act, by holding out the possibility of major funding that would solve all problems and be all things to all people, in effect avoids any consideration of differing interests. It thereby attempts to hold in check any open conflict between city and country, Indian and non-Indian, large-scale operations and more modest family farms. This helps explain why the diversion project has so often been presented as the state's best, if not last, hope, the one thing necessary to guarantee North Dakota's fortunes. In 1962, at the dedication of the Conservancy District headquarters building in Carrington, then Congressman Mark Andrews announced that the consistent flow of water from the diversion "will assure our future" ("Diversion Unit Called 'Greatest'").

Whether the Garrison Diversion Project is a good idea remains the great debating point, the billion-dollar question. But it has been North Dakota's principal idea for obtaining extra federal funds for more than half a century. Many of the battles of numbers between proponents and critics of the Garrison Diversion have been over estimates of the difference the project would make in terms of new factories and farms, equipment and farmers. But the disagreement over those untested, soft figures is shadowed by another set of numbers, the census figures presented at the head of this section. The slight move upward over the past decade is no cause for celebration. The contrast with the figure for 1980—and 1930—is too disturbing, and so is a comparison with the rest of the country. The increase in the 1990s for North Dakota amounts to 0.5 percent, the lowest in all fifty states.

In the end, the Garrison Diversion Project may not be the answer to the population problem—any more than the recurring suggestion that changing the state's name would make a real difference by somehow freeing North Dakota from the burden of remoteness and cold. Even in an age dominated by media images, there are aspects of life that resist control by public relations. Not a single Fortune 500 company is based in North Dakota, and that is not because of the state's image problem.

Or the state's water problems. Without water, there can be no survival. But water alone does not guarantee survival. As a political issue involving water for the state's eastern cities, the Water Resources Act may seem unobjectionable. Proponents and opponents have argued over Garrison for decades using polls, with each side claiming, "The people of North Dakota support us." But who would respond "No" to a question about whether they would like a reliable, high-quality water supply, or whether North Dakota deserves a reasonable share of Missouri River water—or, for that matter, whether they are in favor of protecting wildlife? Responses to such questions prove nothing.

Water quality and water quantity are important issues in the contemporary United States. The tragic aspect of the water issue in North Dakota is that larger trends are at work than a swing of the precipitation pendulum at Devils Lake. It may well prove that the entire Garrison Diversion debate has been a diversion, a distraction from attending to other issues that will prove more challenging and more decisive, such as urbanization and consolidation in the agricultural economy. Water may help sustain population, but stimulating population growth and economic development in the twenty-first century requires much more. The exodus of young people continues. Water is not the answer to that serious problem, which might be put in the form of a flippant question: How are you going to keep 'em down on the farm, or in Fargo, after they've seen MTV? The newsman Eric Sevareid put it in a more personal, wistful fashion: "North Dakota. Why have I not returned for so many years? Why have so few from the prairies ever returned?" (Sevareid, 5).

In a world where powerful trends such as urbanization and globalization are at work, water may well appear the best of all things even if it cannot be, alone, the answer to all the needs of North Dakota. Maybe that explains why the Garrison Diversion as a symbol of North Dakota's struggle is not only once again at the center of a fight, but has been for a good part of the last century, and why the promise of water is affirmed so wholeheartedly by the project's supporters. It is no exaggeration to say that, from the start, they have held onto that promise as if for dear life.

# The McClusky Canal

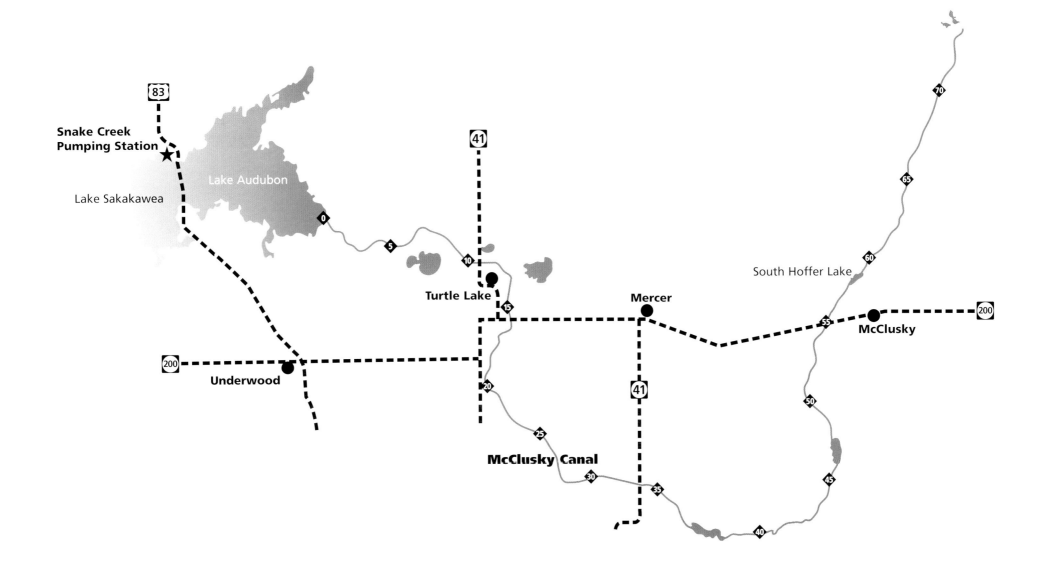

Lake Audubon • **Headwaters**

Headworks • Mile marker 0 • **McClusky Canal**

Mile marker 1 • **McClusky Canal**

Mile marker 11.5 • **McClusky Canal**

Mile marker 13 • **McClusky Canal**

Cross drainage • Mile marker 15 • **McClusky Canal**

Mile marker 17 • **McClusky Canal**

Mile marker 19.5 • **McClusky Canal**

Mile marker 20 • **McClusky Canal**

Mile marker 20.5 • **McClusky Canal**

Slippage • Mile marker 21 • **McClusky Canal**

Mile marker 30 • **McClusky Canal**

Mile marker 29 • **McClusky Canal**

Mile marker 33 • **McClusky Canal**

Source of New Johns Lake • Mile marker 35 • **McClusky Canal**

Mile marker 50 • **McClusky Canal**

Mile marker 48 • **McClusky Canal**

Check structure • Mile marker 55 • **McClusky Canal**

Mile marker 55.2 • **McClusky Canal**

Hoffer Lake • Mile marker 57 • **McClusky Canal**

Hoffer Lake • Mile marker 59 • **McClusky Canal**

Hoffer Lake • Mile marker 59 • **McClusky Canal**

Mile marker 60 • **McClusky Canal**

Drop chute • Mile marker 73.6 • **McClusky Canal**

Drop chute • Mile marker 73.6 • **McClusky Canal**

# Lonetree Wildlife Management Area

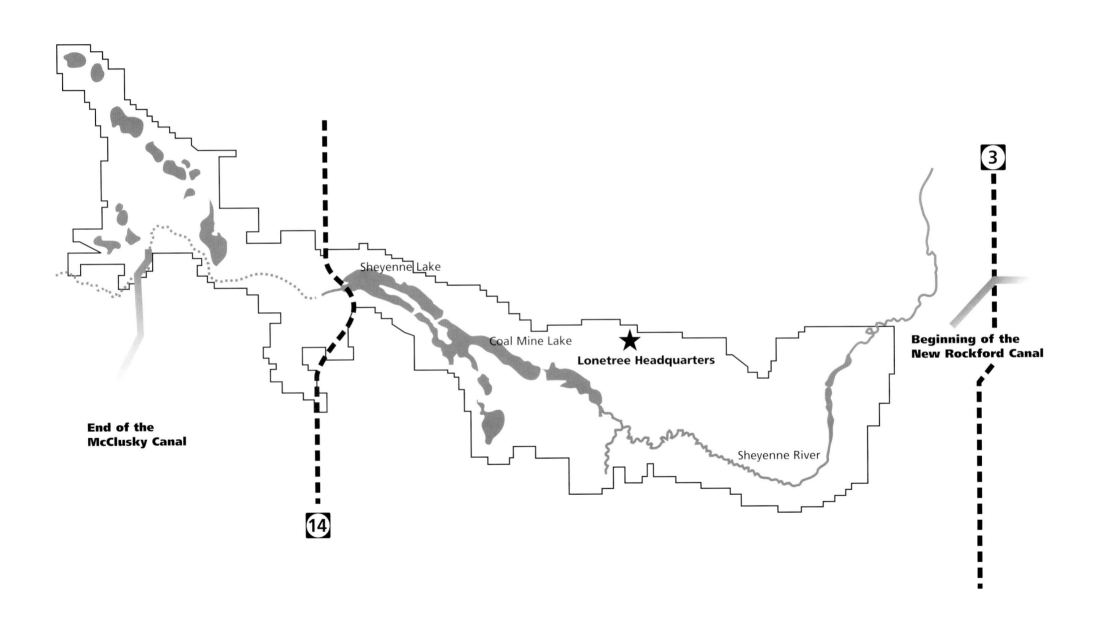

Sheyenne Lake

Coal Mine Lake

★
**Lonetree Headquarters**

**End of the McClusky Canal**

Sheyenne River

**Beginning of the New Rockford Canal**

3

14

Sheyenne Lake on left • **Lonetree Wildlife Management Area**

Coal Mine Lake • **Lonetree Wildlife Management Area**

Coal Mine Lake • **Lonetree Wildlife Management Area**

Coal Mine Lake • **Lonetree Wildlife Management Area**

Coal Mine Lake • **Lonetree Wildlife Management Area**

Sheyenne River • Lonetree Wildlife Management Area

Sheyenne River • **Previously planned site of Lonetree Reservoir Dam**

# New Rockford Canal

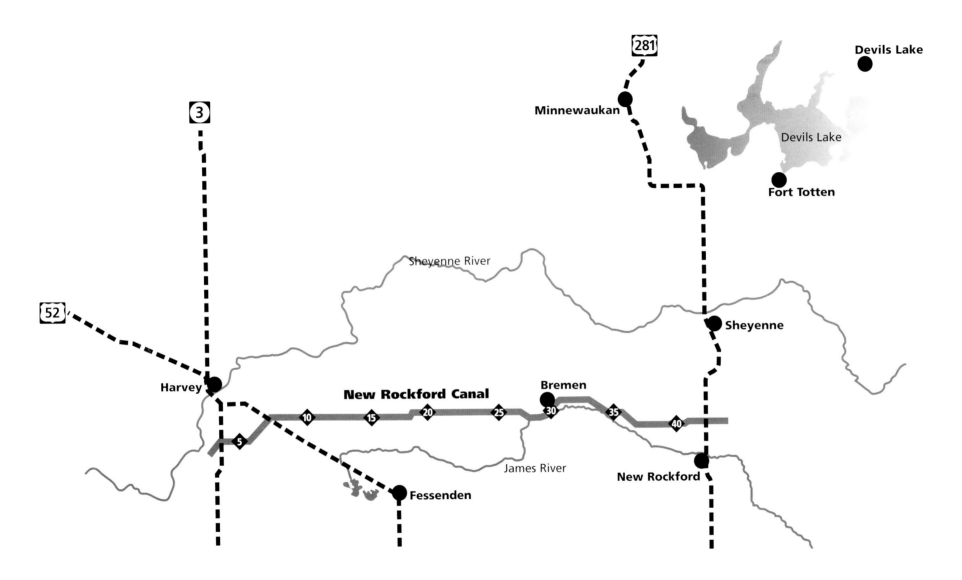

Mile marker 0 • **New Rockford Canal**

Mile marker 1 • **New Rockford Canal**

Mile marker 10 • **New Rockford Canal**

Mile marker 20 • **New Rockford Canal**

Mile marker 26 • **New Rockford Canal**

Mile marker 39.5 • **New Rockford Canal**

Mile marker 42 • **New Rockford Canal**

Mile marker 43 • **New Rockford Canal**

Mile marker 44 • **New Rockford Canal**

Mile marker 44.5 • **New Rockford Canal**

**III** Wayne Gudmundson's photographs of the Garrison Diversion follow the path of the project from one end to the other. They record specific places at specific times, but given the status of the project, they exist in a temporal borderland where past, present, and future coexist. By showing us what might be called contested terrain, the photographs help us understand just what is at issue. That alone is a valuable accomplishment. Perhaps the most startling aspect of the entire diversion controversy is that so few people in North Dakota have ever seen the canals, the waterworks, the land spared in Lonetree from being inundated by the proposed dam and reservoir, or the areas proposed for future development.

No doubt many have seen the Garrison Dam and Lake Sakakawea. Far fewer will have seen Lonetree, and only small numbers from outside the immediate areas will have seen the McClusky and New Rockford canals. The out-of-the-way rural locations of the canals are unlikely sites for a visit; most of the recreational use, Sakakawea and Lonetree aside, is probably by local citizens. A stretch of canal may be a day-trip destination for a resident of Jamestown or Fargo, in search of hunting or fishing or a place for a long trail-bike ride. But such activity is not in the same league as the tourism in the Badlands or at Mt. Rushmore. The Garrison Dam is a monumental structure. Yet if a citizen from outside the immediate vicinity were to drive past the McClusky Canal or the New Rockford Canal by crossing one of the bridges, in many spots the canal would appear more like an ordinary drainage ditch than a grand feat of engineering associated with the expenditure of hundreds of millions of dollars. Except for the stretch where the cut in the McClusky Canal is more than one hundred feet deep, the Garrison Diversion is much more "ditch" than "canal," if one associates "canal" with ships looming above the land in the surreal manner of Suez, or being raised and lowered in giant locks as in Panama. The Garrison Diversion was designed to move water, not boats, although small fishing boats are often visible in Lonetree. Donald Worster writes of the modern irrigation ditch that it reflects "a culture and society built on, and absolutely dependent on, a sharply alienating, intensely managerial relationship with nature. . . . Quite simply, the modern canal, unlike a river, is not an ecosystem. It is simplified, abstracted Water, rigidly separated from the earth and firmly directed to raise food, fill pipes, and make money" (5).

The abstraction is visible in some of the photographs of the Garrison Diversion that show it as part of what Worster calls "a modern hydraulic society" (7). There is an orderliness in these photographs where the canals and waterworks are prominent that some might find reassuring. We see nature brought under control and almost literally put into perspective as the canal is aligned to take us straight to the vanishing point, as if such symmetry and

directness signified that all is right with the world. Yet that precision and order might be anathema to others, who could regard the same photograph as depicting a world stripped of natural forms, of the irregularities and meanderings that mark nature when it is uncontrolled and making its own way, demonstrating the wildness that Henry David Thoreau praised as the preservation of the world. Even in the "natural" areas along the project's course there is a domestication and cultivation of nature. The view may seem unspoiled, but it has been transformed by the plow, by roads, and by selective management of shorelines and vegetation, wildlife and water flow. The landscape has, so to speak, been landscaped.

Gudmundson has been a major photographer of the North Dakota landscape for a long time. The prairie landscape, he says, "is what I grew up looking at." His respect and affection for it are everywhere evident, in his lyrical sense of its moods and his clear-eyed awareness of its power. With his panoramic images, he captures the sweep and openness of the land. With his superb printing, he renders the scenes in subtle tones and with exacting particularity. Even when he photographs the not-yet-completed water project, his North Dakota is a place of grand vistas of land and sky, given an intimate feeling by a human scale and a delicacy that keep the landscape relatively free of melodrama. His images are handsomely composed, yet many retain the informal feeling of views seen on a relaxed, ordinary journey rather than exceptional once-in-a-lifetime sights. As a group, they demonstrate a steady, thoughtful observation. Signs of human activity, especially those associated with the Diversion Project, are at the center of Gudmundson's concern. But he cannot resist being fascinated by the procession of clouds in the sky, the trees that break the horizon line, the vegetation that shoots up in the foreground—all the myriad elements of a world that draws him in, and through his photographs, us.

Since the canals are not under construction now, little of the rawness of the building phase is revealed, although the photograph of construction near the Garrison Dam, with the earthmoving equipment silhouetted against the sky, establishes what it is like when it does occur. As an interim report, these images come after the changes imposed by the Diversion Project, and long after the initial transformation of prairie and river bottom into cultivated land. Yet in many images the distinction between nature and human civilization seems clear. Along some stretches, notably in Lonetree, the landscape is picturesque, a scene of rural recreation that suggests an unchanging, innocent pastoral world. The images made in those spots contrast sharply with the images of the canals and waterworks, where the hand of man is unmistakable. Those alternatives define the overall vision, yet not in terms of a simple moralistic opposition. The canals can seem cold and intrusive or dynamic and heroic, while images of the Wildlife Management Area can seem harmonious or disquieting. The winter scenes in particular suggest both brilliance and desolation, the grandeur and the cold. The opening image can provide an invitation to ice fishing, or a reminder that picnic season is far away and it might be best to turn one's thoughts homeward.

Given the basic elements of the Diversion Project, the pictorial challenge is apparent. After all, what can one do with a canal? Moving top to bottom, side to side, or at a diagonal, the canal segments make their appearance as Gudmundson works his changes, but not as a set of mechanical variations. The arrangements of sky, land, and water can appear romantic, as in the majestic shot on the cover of this book, in which the water and the roads along the sides lead directly toward the horizon. Even that scene, however, is haunted by emptiness and inaction. The ends of the waterway appear sealed, there are no vehicles on the roads, and the banks show signs of patching with riprap. That photograph has a complement at the current end of the journey, where the New Rockford Canal takes one final turn and snubs up against the bank, ending neither with a bang nor a whimper but with a whisper, as a quiet pool in a field, awaiting its fate.

If the initial image, alone, could almost serve as a publicity shot for the Garrison Diversion Conservancy District, an image of apparent harmony between the natural and the human, there are also images that suggest the disruption caused by the canal. These images reveal dead ends and disjunctions, a jagged landscape where drainage pipes can appear anywhere but always seem out of place, sprouting at odd angles out of the land. Roads do not follow smooth, direct paths but cut across the physical landscape—and the pictorial space—introducing barriers into the landscape. Foreground and background are separated, so that in several shots there is no easy path to the farms in the distance. Instead of seeing the comforting irregularity of the shore in the Lonetree, we are confronted by something more disturbing, if pictorially complex. This landscape of disconnection goes against the grand theme of the Diversion Project as a whole, designed above all as an instrument of connection but not connecting, at least not yet.

There is something thrilling about the hard-edged angularity of the spillway, moving down in giant's steps right at our feet and then shooting to the horizon, a demonstration of the intended use of elevation for gravity flow. But the cumulative effect of moving along the path of the Diversion Project from west to east is less than exhilarating. The most dramatic structures appear mainly on the McClusky Canal, which comes first, but along the canals proper there are no trees, only casual growth such as cattails and the evenly mowed sides of the canal. The canals and waterworks are shown as not in use, with no human presence and no obvious purpose: the water is not shown fulfilling John Wesley Powell's vision, shooting out of a pivot rig or pouring into the Red River. The air of a dry gulch in some of the New Rockford Canal sections suggests abandonment, a quality not conducive to inspiring anticipation for the heralded day when water will flow.

The Garrison Diversion was never planned as a scenic wonder. It was meant to be a water-conveyance system, or, as Helen Correll puts it, "a gigantic plumbing project" (2). The project claims our attention as a photographic subject because of its scale and scope, and because it is open to sight. Who would find a buried water pipe interesting? Many photographers have been fascinated by the striking forms created by modern industry, seduced by the purist, powerful geometry even though the resulting photographs may tell us little of the real workings of industrialism. The cover of the first issue of *Life* magazine in 1936 featured one of Margaret Bourke-White's signature photographs, a depiction of the monumental forms of the Fort Peck Dam. Gudmundson's photograph of the spillway resembles such epic imagery. There are contemporary photographers who have rendered construction sites and industrial structures as deadpan, even ironic subjects, where the offhand, irregular distribution of building materials or the neat geometry of industrial-park architecture plays off more heroic images. Gudmundson is too much of a traditionalist for that.

He is also too determined to be fair-minded. "Balance" is a key term in his vocabulary, and it refers to politics and personal behavior as well as to pictorial composition. His photographs are the product neither of easy irony, rendering the canals and waterworks as monstrous intrusions, nor of propagandistic advocacy, covering the same ground—and water—in the opposite direction by making the project look as noble as Yosemite in the photographs of Ansel Adams. The images present a complex composite. The response invited is not so much simple admiration or antagonism as a concentrated attention; the photographs seem to say, "Here's what it looks like. Now what do you think?" There would be many other ways of making photographs of the project—for instance, as a series of portraits. But as a landscape photographer, Gudmundson is committed to representing the subject through the landscape and what it reveals. These photographs are not "pure landscape photography"—if such a thing exists—for there is no escaping the historical and political context. Ben Schatz's billboard may have come down long ago, but a cattle-crossing bridge or a fisherman at Lonetree can also serve as a reminder of the controversy.

The photographs do what photographs do best: reveal the visible. The selection of sites and sights is necessarily reductive, since it would take a tremendous effort to photograph the entire strip from the Garrison Dam to the end of the New Rockford Canal. Yet Gudmundson's record is also expansive, because it sets key points such as the deep cut in the McClusky Canal alongside less exceptional ones from Lonetree and elsewhere to suggest the range of landscapes along the Garrison Diversion's path, and because it establishes a linkage, with each photograph stretching out to meet the next even if the canals are not always shown running from side to side in a neat horizontal band. But the record still is incomplete, only hinting at what exists outside the frame, beyond the horizon, in Fargo or on some farm where the water ultimately might be used.

Maps, economic tables, scientific charts, and records of congressional debates may present some kinds of information better than photographs. But photography is unrivaled when it comes to using representation to establish a sense of presence and a sense of place, to make us feel as if we are viewing a scene directly when we are only looking at an image. An important demonstration of the power of documentary photography, the Gudmundson photographs testify to what has been built and what has been left alone, what has changed and what has not. As a segmented series, they fix attention on individual scenes and also establish a counterpoint between specific images and between single images and the overall sequence. The journey across North Dakota from the great dam to the quiet field, from the digging equipment silhouetted against the sky to the tree elegantly reflected in the last stretch of canal, follows a continuous trajectory in space, from west to east. It is not a continuous journey in time, however, since it encompasses not only all four seasons but also, in effect, the years, decades, and more that shaped the land in the process Deborah Bright refers to when she notes the "human values and actions imposed on the land over time."

Viewing the photographs, it is at times hard to recall that this terrain has been contested, the subject of an intense political struggle. No protesters with placards line the canal. In some of the photographs, as in many images of the American West, there is a sense of dreamland, of an uninhabited preserve removed from the modern world. But that air of detachment is illusory. The Garrison project remains physically at the heart of the state and symbolically at the center of its history over many decades, its current situation, and, though in different ways for advocates and critics, its future.

If Garrison is as necessary as its proponents claim, then these pictures reveal the heroic framework for a largely hidden source of salvation, just waiting to be brought to life through an infusion of water. If Garrison is as unnecessary as its opponents claim, then these pictures reveal the residue of foolish dreams, the immense but wasteful product of a misguided attempt to control nature using inappropriate if impressive means that will not lead to any promised land. Wayne Gudmundson's photographs employ no calculated ambiguity, yet with their complex sense of balance they manage to acknowledge the opposing points of view while transcending them both.

*Works Cited*

Bright, Deborah. "On Mother Nature and Marlboro Men: An Inquiry into the Cultural Meanings of Landscape Photography." In *The Contest of Meaning*, ed. Richard Bolton. Cambridge, Mass.: MIT Press, 1989, 125–42.

Carrels, Peter. *Uphill Against Water: The Great Dakota Water War*. Lincoln: University of Nebraska Press, 1999.

Cooper, Vernon. "Garrison Diversion: A Project for All North Dakotans." *North Dakota Quarterly* 35, no. 3 (summer 1967): 72–77.

Correll, Helen Hoehn. "Until the Old Men Die: A Case Study of the Garrison Diversion Project in North Dakota." Ph.D. diss., Michigan Technological University, 2000.

"Diversion Unit Called 'Greatest'." *North Dakota Water Users Association News Bulletin* 12, no. 6 (October–November 1972): 30.

Doemel, Nancy J., with preface and concluding observations by Lynton K. Caldwell. *The Garrison Diversion Unit: Science, Technology, Politics, Values*. Bloomington: Indiana University Institute for Science, Technology, and Public Policy, 1979.

Dominy, Floyd. "Dominy: Dakotas on Verge of Greatest Era in History." Unidentified newspaper clipping, n.d. [February 4, 1966?]. Garrison Diversion clipping file, State Historical Society of North Dakota Archives.

Dunne, Peter Finley. *Mr. Dooley on Ivrything and Ivrybody*. New York: Dover, 1963.

Garrison Diversion Conservancy District Web site, www.garrisondiv.org.

Gottlieb, Robert. *A Life of Its Own: The Politics and Power of Water*. San Diego: Harcourt Brace Jovanovich, 1988.

Harvey, Mark W. T. "North Dakota, the Northern Plains, and the Missouri Valley Authority." *North Dakota History* 59, no. 3 (summer 1992): 28–39.

"Hearings at Devils Lake." Brochure, 1957. Garrison Diversion clipping file, State Historical Society of North Dakota Archives.

Jacobs, Mike. "The Garrison Diversion Project Is North Dakota's History and Destiny." *High Country News* 16 (September 17, 1984): 1, 10–11.

Josephy, Alvin J., Jr. "Dr. Strangelove Builds a Canal." *Audubon* 77, no. 2 (March 1975): 76–84, 86–87, 90, 92–94, 100, 104–5, 110–12.

Kelly, Paul Edward. "Under the Ditch: Irrigation and the Garrison Diversion Controversy." Master's thesis, North Dakota State University, 1989.

Works Cited (continued)

Kurian, Priya A. and Robert V. Bartlett. "The Garrison Diversion Dream and the Politics of Landscape Engineering." *North Dakota History* 59, no. 3 (summer 1992): 40–51.

Leitch, Jay A. and Mariah J. Tenamoc, eds. *Science and Policy: Interbasin Water Transfer of Aquatic Biota.* Fargo: Institute for Regional Studies, North Dakota State University, 2001.

[Limvere, Karl, and Richard Madson.] "Garrison Diversion: Rumblings on the Ditch." *North Dakota Union Farmer* 18 (July 1972): 4–18.

Miller, James Nathan. "Half a Billion Dollars down the Drain." *Reader's Digest*, November 1976, 143–48.

Pearson, Gary L. "The Dakota Water Resources Act of 1998: Retrofitting a 19th-Century Dream to 21st-Century Reality." Presented at the North Dakota Chapter of the Soil and Water Conservation Society Annual Meeting, Jamestown, December 3, 1998.

Pindar. *The Odes of Pindar*, trans. Richmond Lattimore. 2nd ed. Chicago: University of Chicago Press, 1976.

"Procedures for the Purchase of Land and Right of Way." U.S. Bureau of Reclamation, n.d. "Farmers . . . Records," Farmers Canal Protesters Association Records, State Historical Society of North Dakota Archives.

Reisner, Marc. *Cadillac Desert: The American West and Its Disappearing Water.* Revised and updated. New York: Penguin, 1993.

Robinson, Elwyn B. *History of North Dakota.* Lincoln: University of Nebraska Press, 1966.

Russell, Brian Keith. "Promise of Water: The Legacy of Pick-Sloan and the Irrigation of North Dakota." Report of the North Dakota Humanities Council, February 2002.

Sevareid, Eric. *Not So Wild a Dream.* New York: Atheneum, 1976.

Sherwood, Glen. *New Wounds for Old Prairies.* Pequot Lakes, Minn.: Country Printing, 1972.

Thorson, John E. *River of Promise, River of Peril: The Politics of Managing the Missouri River.* Lawrence: University Press of Kansas, 1994.

"Young: Diversion in Deep Trouble." *Jamestown (N.Dak.) Sun*, January 17, 1974, 1.

Wilkins, Robert P., and Wynona Huchette Wilkins. *North Dakota: A Bicentennial History.* New York: W. W. Norton for the American Association for State and Local History, 1977.

Worster, Donald. *Rivers of Empire: Water, Aridity, and the Growth of the American West.* New York: Oxford University Press, 1992.


All statements by Wayne Gudmundson and Richard Madson are from conversations with the author. The Pindar is the opening line of the First Olympian Ode, in Pindar, 1. The Twain statement is quoted in Gottlieb, 272. The Bright quotation is from "On Mother Nature and Marlboro Men," 126.

## Acknowledgments

We would like express our gratitude to many individuals and institutions for making this project possible. We are deeply appreciative of the hospitality, openness, and cooperation shown to a pair of Minnesotans.

First and foremost, we must thank the State Historical Society of North Dakota for sponsoring the exhibition and the Institute for Regional Studies at North Dakota State University for sponsoring this publication. In Bismarck, we wish to offer special thanks to Claudia Berg, Director of Curatorial and Exhibit Services; Lotte Bailey, Deputy State Archivist; and Shawn Holz, Curator of Exhibits. In Fargo, we must thank Tom Riley, Dean of the College of the Humanities and director of the institute; and Tom Isern, Professor of History and editor at the institute. We are also grateful to the North Dakota Art Gallery Association for agreeing to tour the exhibition. In Moorhead, our special thanks go to Al Sheets for his dedicated and skillful work on the design of this book.

At the Garrison Diversion Conservancy District main office in Carrington, we were aided by Warren L. Jamison, Manager, and Maria Effertz Hanson, Director of Communications. We also received help from the staff at the McClusky office.

On the other side, so to speak, we are grateful to Dr. Gary Pearson and Richard Madson for providing information and materials.

At the U.S. Bureau of Reclamation in Bismarck, Charles Vasicek enabled us to review the photographic archives, and Mike Morahl offered information about the canal maintenance efforts.

Quinn-Louise Cheney, Political and Economic Relations Officer at the Canadian Consulate General, Minneapolis, provided information about the current attitude of the Canadian government toward the Garrison Diversion Project.

Mike Eggl, Economic Development Specialist in the Bismarck office of U.S. Senator Byron Dorgan, provided us with a copy of the North Dakota Water Resources Act.

Al Hovland, Michelle Hengel, and Paul L'Heureux at aha! Al Hovland Advertising provided assistance with the maps, and Henry E. Weddington of the U.S. Army Corps of Engineers and Gary Redmann of the North Dakota Department of Transportation helped clear the way for use of photographs.

Mike Jacobs, editor of the *Grand Forks Herald*, and Professor Mark Harvey of North Dakota State University, Fargo, were kind enough to read an early draft of the text and make many helpful comments. Of course, they bear no responsibility for errors in matters of fact or interpretation in the final version. Phil Freshman provided editorial expertise.

Before we set out to drive the length of the canals one Sunday afternoon, John and Carol Sellie provided an excellent brunch and discussed with us the development and long-term effects of the New Rockford Canal. Nick Faul was good enough to meet with Rob Silberman and discuss his family's experience as farmers whose land was taken for the proposed Lonetree Reservoir and Dam but is now part of the Lonetree Wildlife Management Area. Todd and Mary Goven provided information about their farm, which originally belonged to Todd's parents, and the impact of the McClusky Canal.

Wayne's fieldwork on this project was made possible by a pair of awards. He would like to thank Minnesota State University Moorhead for a faculty research grant and the McKnight Foundation for a photography fellowship.

Rob would like to thank the Dean's Office of the College of Liberal Arts at the University of Minnesota for a research grant that helped support his work on this project.

For support and advice along the way, Wayne would like to thank Jane Edwards Gudmundson, and Rob would like to thank Anedith Nash.

**Wayne Gudmundson** was born in Fargo, North Dakota, in 1949. His photographs have appeared in seven other books. He is project director and editor of the Prairie Documents Photographic Book Series. His work is in several permanent collections, including the Museum of Modern Art, New York; the San Francisco Museum of Modern Art; the PaineWebber Collection, New York; the Canadian Centre for Architecture, Montreal; the U.S. Embassy, Reykjavik, Iceland; and Ralph's Corner Bar in Moorhead, Minnesota. Gudmundson teaches photography at Minnesota State University Moorhead and is acting director of New Rivers Press, Moorhead.

**Robert Silberman** is Associate Professor of Art History at the University of Minnesota, Minneapolis, where he regularly teaches the history of photography. He served as senior advisor for the 1999 PBS series *American Photography: A Century of Images* and, with Vicki Goldberg, coauthored the companion volume of the same title. He writes on photography, film, contemporary art, and craft for a variety of publications and has received several awards for his critical writing. He has also curated several exhibitions, including *World Views: Maps and Art* in 1999 at the Frederick R. Weisman Art Museum, University of Minnesota, Minncapolis.

The existing end of the New Rockford Canal

The existing end of the New Rockford Canal